D0578146

WITHDRAWN

BICYCLES

After the wheels are built, they are moved to another part of the factory, where they will be attached to bicycle frames.

Arlene Erlbach

Lerner Publications Company • Minneapolis

Dedicated to Charlie, Scratchy, Robbie, Charade, Sparkey, and Dusty, who wait so quietly; and a special dedication to Chelsea Chereé Sutter and Eric Edmund Sutter—A. E.

Illustrated by Jackie Urbanovic

Words printed in **bold** are explained in the glossary on pages 43 and 44.

Library of Congress Cataloging-in-Publication Data

Erlbach, Arlene.
Bicycles/by Arlene Erlbach.
p. cm.—(How it's made)
Includes index.
ISBN 0-8225-2388-4
1. Bicycles—Juvenile literature. [1. Bicycles and bicycling.] I. Title.
II. Series: Erlbach, Arlene. How it's made.
TL410.E75 1994 93-34457
629.227'2—dc20 CIP
AC

Manufactured in the United States of America

1 2 3 4 5 6 - I/JR - 99 98 97 96 95 94

CONTENTS

In the United States alone, about 20 million kids cycle more than once a week.

1

From Fast Feet to Safety Bike

They're the healthiest way to get around, besides walking. They don't pollute. Kids don't need a license to ride them. Hooray for bicycles!

More than 500 million people in the world zoom along on bikes. About a third of these bicycles belong to kids. If you lined up every child's bicycle end to end, they'd form 10 bicycle parades around the earth!

Even though a bike is something most American kids own or will own, the first bicycles weren't designed for children at all. A French inventor built the first bicycle in 1791, for adults. Bicycles became popular throughout Europe, but because each bicycle was made by hand, they were very expensive. Only the richest people could afford to buy them.

That first bike didn't look like the one you ride. It had a heavy wooden frame shaped like a horse or lion. It didn't have pedals, so the rider moved it by pushing his or her feet along the ground. It didn't have brakes, either, and it couldn't be steered. Going uphill was very tiring. And a ride downhill could be thrilling—or dangerous.

The first bicycle was called a Célérifère—that's French for "fast feet." The Célérifère was certainly faster than walking, and it had an advantage over a horse—it didn't need to be fed. In those days, cars hadn't been invented yet.

This bike was made out of heavy iron and wood. It had a front wheel a little over three feet high, and its seat was mounted on a spring. All this added up to a bumpy, wobbly ride. So people called this bike the Boneshaker.

In 1817 a German inventor built a bicycle with a padded seat, and with handlebars attached to the front wheel. The handlebars allowed this new bike to be steered. Then, in about 1860, a bicycle was invented that had pedals attached to cranks on its front wheel. Finally, people could ride a bike without scraping their feet on the ground. But bicycles were still very heavy and tiring to ride.

Bikes like these became so common that people started calling them Ordinaries. They weren't very safe. But they rode more smoothly than the Boneshaker. Ordinaries had rubber tires cemented to their wheel rims.

As people learned more about bikes, they discovered something important. The bigger the front wheel, the faster the bike moved. By 1870 bikes had front wheels from four to five feet high. The back wheels measured about a foot and a half. It was difficult for riders to get on and off the bike's high seat. A fall from this bike could cause serious injury, or even death.

Even though they weren't safe, these bicycles with the huge front wheels were lighter and easier to ride than any other kind of bike. Companies began to make these new bikes in large quantities, and more people than ever before owned their own bicycles.

As an alternative to the big-wheeled bikes, some manufacturers made giant tricycles—bicycles with three wheels. These satisfied the adults who were afraid of riding two-wheeled bikes, and children, too—at least for a while. Then, in 1890, a bike called the Safety came along and changed bicycles forever.

The Safety had two wheels the same size, just like your bike does. It used a **chain drive** like yours, too—pedal cranks were attached to a large **sprocket** surrounded by a chain. The pedals turned the large sprocket, which moved the chain. The chain then pulled a smaller sprocket that moved the back wheel and powered the bike. The chain and sprockets made the Safety easy to ride.

By 1895 the new Safety was being called the bicycle. This word comes from the Latin words bi-, *meaning "two," and* cycle, *meaning "wheels." Your bike is a lighter, more modern version of the Safety.*

- Mountain bikes are the most popular type of bicycle in the United States.
- About one out of every three Americans owns a bicycle. About half of these owners are kids.
- Bicycle racing became an Olympic event in 1896.
- Worldwide, about 100 million bicycles are manufactured every year.

Within a few years, **pneumatic (noo-MAT-ik) tires**—tires filled with air—were added to the bicycle. Bicycles became even more comfortable to ride. Soon another inventor came up with **coaster brakes,** which stopped the bike when the rider backpedaled.

The bike craze spread throughout the world, and bicycling became an international sport. By 1910 more than one million Americans owned a bike.

Now bicycles are made in large factories. They are shipped to stores like bike shops, department stores, or discount houses. They come in a variety of sizes, colors, and styles. But no matter what kind of bike you have, it started with an idea that's more than 200 years old.

Want to learn more about how ideas turn into bicycles? Then read on!

2
Design

Almost every year, major bike companies make changes to the models they sell. They might make a certain bike lighter or faster. Maybe they'll use different metals to build it. Or maybe they'll make a bike's tires thinner or wider. You may not notice the changes in bikes from year to year. But bike stores do. They want to have the latest models to sell to new customers.

Each idea for a new bicycle starts in the design department of the bike factory. A person called a designer or mechanical engineer begins by sketching pictures with pencil and paper.

Fashions change from year to year, in bicycle design as well as in clothes and accessories.

After the designer has sketched the bike, he or she draws it again, this time on a special kind of computer. The computer is attached to a special pad and pen called a digitizer pad and a digitizer pen. Together they make up an electronic drawing board.

When the designer moves the digitizer pen across the pad, the computer picks up signals from the pad. Three-dimensional pictures appear on the screen. This process of drawing is called CAD—short for **Computer-Aided Design.** The CAD picture can be printed, with a special kind of printer called a plotter. This picture will be used to make a **blueprint,** or a diagram, of the bicycle.

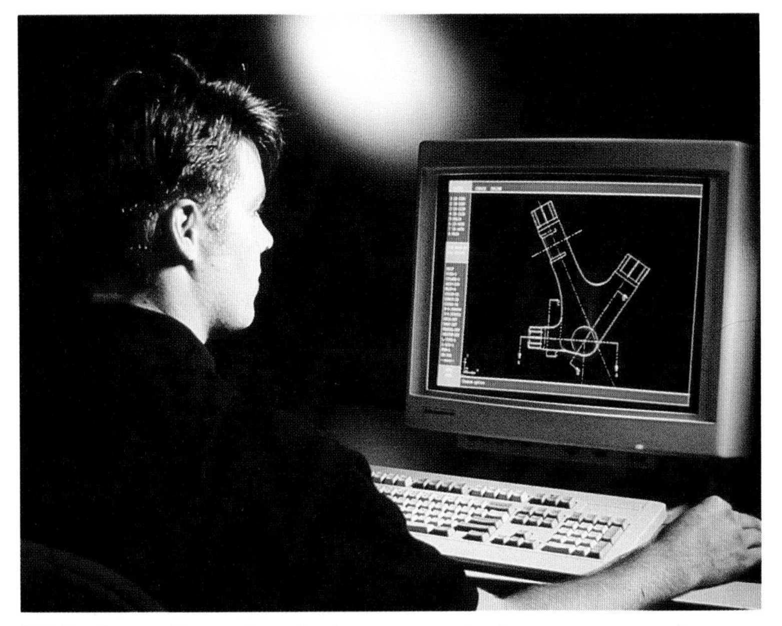

With three-dimensional pictures, a designer can see how a bicycle will look after it has been built. This type of drawing is also used by people who design new cars, trucks, and airplanes.

Next, somebody in another part of the factory follows the blueprints to build several **prototypes.** Prototypes are the first samples of the bike, which are tested to see if they will hold up to heavy riding. Sometimes a prototype is attached to a machine that imitates a person riding it. This machine actually shakes the bike about a million times—that's two weeks of continuous rattling. Another machine squeezes and pulls on the bike's frame for hours.

In another test, some of the factory employees might take prototypes outside and ride them. Or, sometimes, a bicycle factory will hire people who live nearby to try out the bikes. But the riders don't take a bicycle that has been on a machine. These bikes may no longer be safe to ride, and they certainly wouldn't feel like new bikes. Then, if the prototype rides well, thousands of that model will be manufactured for sale.

- In the 1890s, some school districts didn't allow teachers to ride bikes to school.
- Some churches frowned on riding to church, too.
- There are more bicycles in China than in any other country. Eighty percent of travel in China is done by bicycle.

PARTS OF A BICYCLE

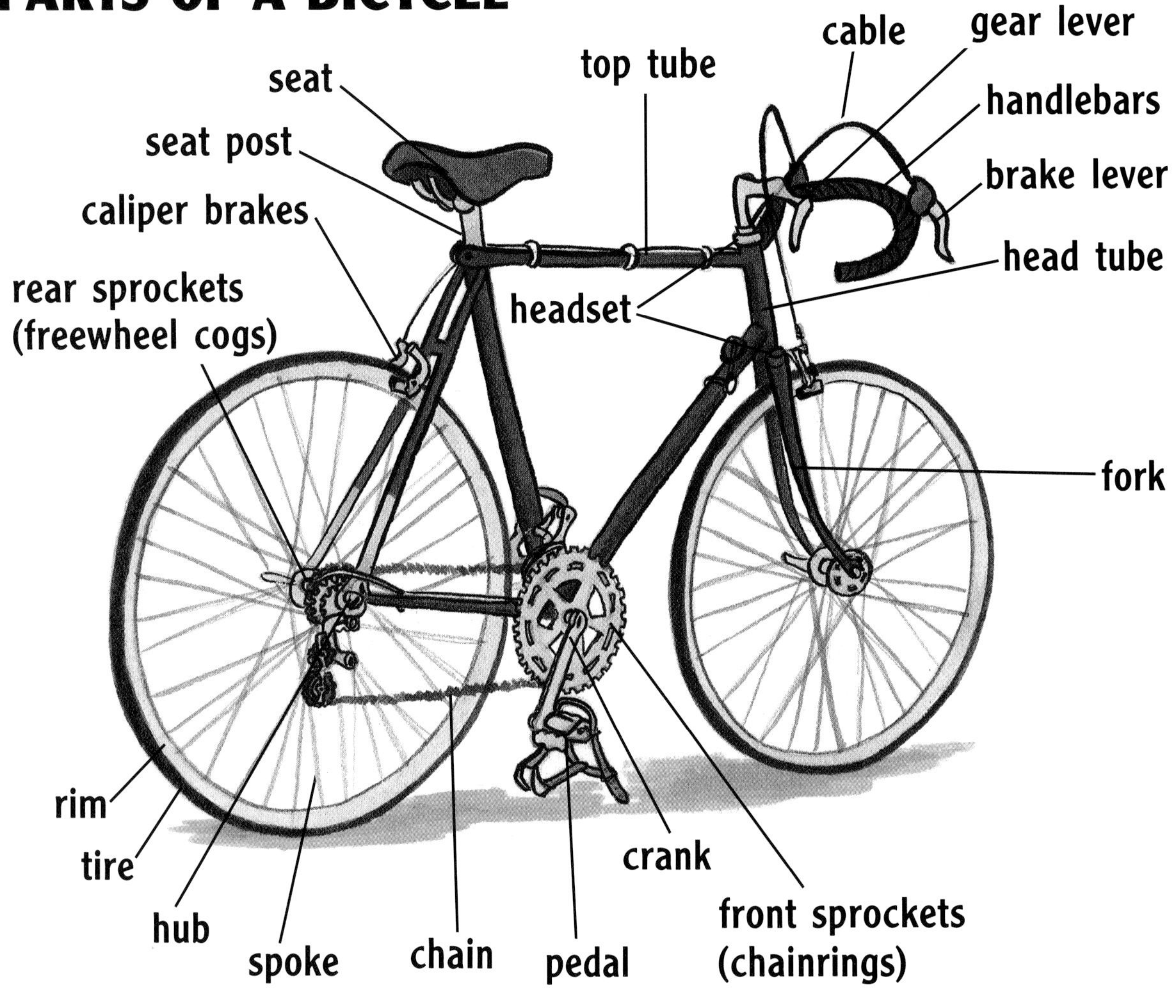

3

Frames

The first step in building a bicycle is making the frame. Long steel or aluminum tubes are cut into various lengths and joined to make frames. A moving belt called a conveyor belt carries the tubes to the tube cutoff machine, and one by one, the tubes are pushed through the machine. Rollers inside the machine make the tubes spin in place as a blade slices each one to the correct length. The cut tubes fall into a basket.

Next the tubes are notched so that they will fit together well. The saw blade cuts curved slices into the tubes' ends.

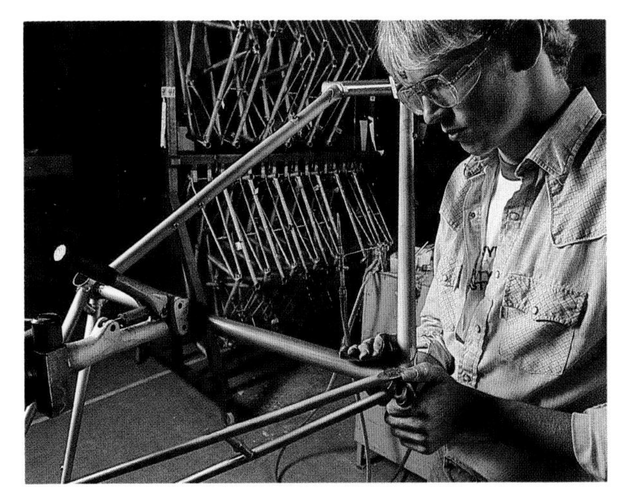

The frame is the bicycle's skeleton. All the other parts of the bike are attached to it, so the frame needs to be especially strong.

The frame's tubes are **welded** together, often with robotic devices. Robotic welders don't look like humans, as robots in movies sometimes do. Robotic welders are machines that work with the help of people who operate them.

First a machine operator clamps two tubes that have to be joined. Weldfiller wire, a thin metal thread, comes off a huge spool and is fed into the robotic welder. Two torches move toward the spot where the tubes join together. The weldfiller wire melts over the joint, where it will harden. Then that section goes to another machine operator, and another robotic welder, to have another tube added. The unfinished frame goes from worker to worker, and robot to robot, until it is complete.

Your bicycle's **fork**—the part that holds the front wheel to the bike—is made in the factory's framebuilding department, too. It's made by welding together sections of thinner tubes.

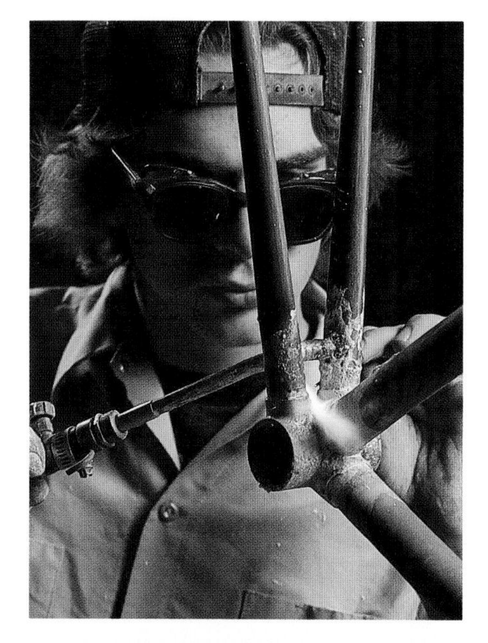

Top: *Welding a bicycle frame by hand.*
Bottom: *A robotic welder.*

Once the frame is complete, it needs to be inspected. A metal ball is pushed through the seat tube to force out any bits of metal from inside. Then a metal stick is pushed through the seat tube to make sure the tube is clear.

A worker also makes sure that the frame's tubes are lined up properly. He or she clamps the frame to a straightening table and measures it with special blocks. If the tubes do not line up right, the worker bends them with a crowbar until they are straight.

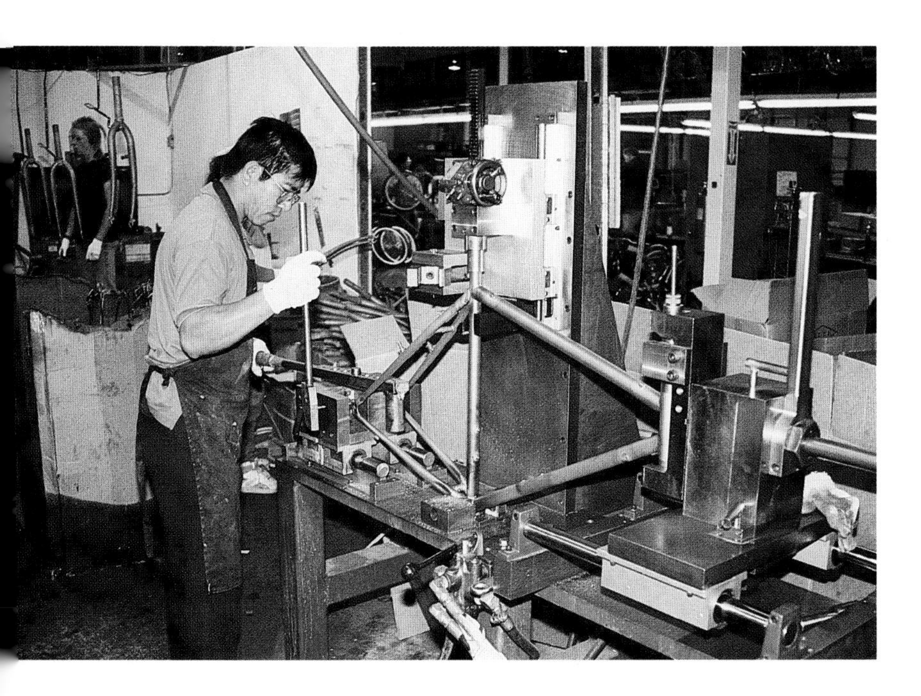

A frame must be perfectly straight before any other parts are attached to it.

In one of the final steps of framebuilding, the joints on the frame and fork are sanded so they'll be smooth. Then bearing cups, or rings, are installed into the top tube and the fork. These cups contain the **ball bearings** that make the bike steer easily. They are located right underneath a bike's handlebars.

Now each frame and its fork are hung on a moving overhead rack. The parts are on their way to the factory's paint department to have color applied.

After the joints are sanded, bicycle frames are easier to paint. It's also important that the joints don't scratch the rider.

4

Painting

Painting is very important to a bike frame. Paint protects the metal so that it won't rust. And color is very important to you as a shopper. A bicycle's color is one of the main reasons a customer chooses a particular bike.

Each year's new models sport new colors. Bright primary colors might be the rage one year, and neon pastels the next. Maybe the new colors will only be slightly lighter or darker than the year before. Even so, most kids want to buy their new bikes in the latest color.

The most popular bike colors change from year to year.

If the frames are washed well, the paint will go on smoothly.

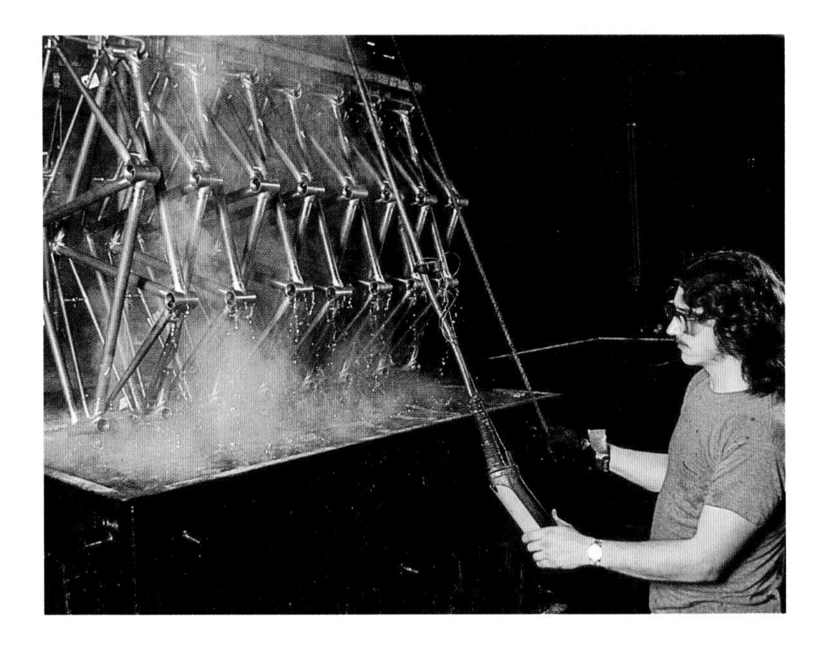

First a water and chemical solution rinses any dust or oil from the frames. Then the frames enter a drying oven for a few minutes. Now they are ready for the first coat of paint.

Sometimes a powdered paint is applied with robotic sprayers. The paint goes on as a dusty, fine powder. When it's exposed to heat in a baking oven, the paint melts and spreads to make a strong, shiny coat.

When the paint is dried, a worker adds decals, such as company logos or colorful stripes. Decals are made of strong paper with a very sticky back.

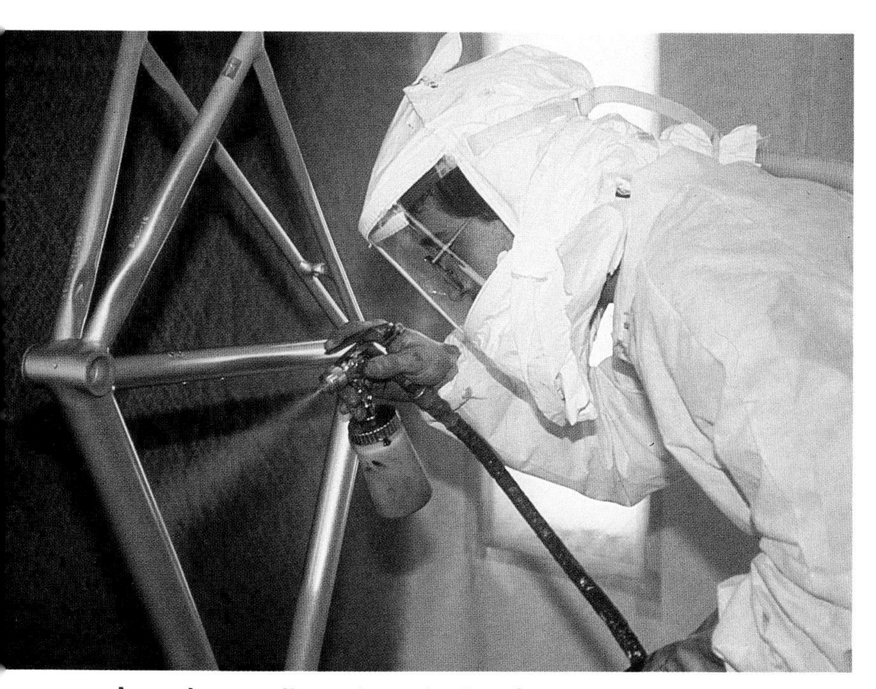

A worker applies primer by hand.

If liquid paint is used, the first coat is called a **primer.** It's usually a grayish white color. The primer prepares the frame for the colored paint. It smoothes the surface and helps the colored paint stick. Without the primer, the color coat might flake and peel.

Primer may be applied by hand or by industrial robots. A fine mist of paint is squirted onto the frame. The mist is so fine that it's almost invisible. But when it goes on the bike, or if it gets on a person's clothes or skin, it can be seen—well! So the people who work with the paint wear protective clothing. Masks prevent them from inhaling paint fumes.

After the primer goes on, the frames are dried in a drying oven. Then the color coat is applied, by robots, and later touched up by hand. A worker uses a spray gun to paint the joints and corners that the robots can't reach.

The frames go through the oven again to dry the colored coat. If this method of painting is used, decals are added now. These decals are made of very delicate paper or plastic. A final clear coat of paint is applied, to protect the decals and to make the bike look shiny.

Finally, a serial number is stamped onto the bike. A bike owner can register his or her bike with a local police department. If the bike is ever stolen, the police use the serial number to identify it.

Frames and forks are hung on an overhead rack and sent through a drying oven.

5

Wheels

A bicycle wheel has five main parts: the **rim,** the **hub,** the **spokes,** the tire, and the inner tube. Putting a wheel together takes many steps. They all take place in a part of the bicycle factory called wheelbuilding.

First the metal frame called the rim is formed. Rims begin as huge rolls of thin metal strips. The strips are measured to the correct size and cut with a saw. Then another machine curls each strip's ends and welds them together. But the rim isn't perfectly round yet. It looks like an elongated O.

The rim enters a machine called a first-former. Rollers inside the first-former curl the edges of the rim a bit. Then the rim goes into a machine called a final-former, which molds the rim into a circle and crimps and seals the edges so they look like the top of a tin can. The edges are tight and firm, and they will hold in the tire later.

- Wilbur and Orville Wright were bicycle makers. The Wright brothers designed the first airplane in their bicycle shop.
- The top tube on a girl's bike was dropped in the 1880s to accommodate long skirts that women wore.
- Girls' bikes are much less popular than they once were. Most girls wear pants when they ride bikes, and they don't need the dropped bar.

Next the rims are drilled with holes, for the spokes to be inserted. A worker puts the unfinished rim in a machine called a punch press. The rim sits inside a groove while sharp points punch out holes. The press quickly punches out all the holes at once. It only takes a few seconds to punch a rim. After the rim is punched, another worker checks that the holes are positioned correctly and completely cut.

From the punch press, the rim goes to a sizing machine. The sizing machine has different sizes of round, metal layers, like a tall wedding cake. Each layer is designed for a certain size rim. The sizing machine pushes and expands the rim so that it becomes perfectly round.

A worker laces a wheel. This job demands very precise work. Each spoke must go into the correct hole and in the right direction.

In a trip to the paint department, the rim is painted or plated with **chrome.** Then the rim is returned to wheelbuilding to become part of the finished wheel.

Next a worker "laces" the wheel, which means he or she puts the spokes into the holes in the hub. When the spokes are properly placed, they hold the rim tight so the wheel will roll well. The end of each spoke is grooved like a screw. The person lacing the wheel screws the ends in the holes and attaches tiny nuts, called nipples, to each end of the spokes. Another machine tightens the nuts so the spokes won't loosen.

A worker trues a wheel. A computerized device helps the worker make the correct measurements.

The wheel is nearly complete. But first the tires and inner tubes need to be installed. One worker begins by inserting a partially inflated inner tube into the tire. Then a second worker sets the tube and tire onto the rim. A third person fully inflates the tire and checks its air pressure.

The very last step in wheelbuilding is **truing** the wheel, or making sure it doesn't wobble. The person who trues the wheel checks that the spokes grip the rim properly and that the wheel is perfectly round. Then, if the wheel checks out, it's ready to be attached to a bicycle frame.

6

Putting It All Together

Wheels, frames, and forks are usually the only bicycle parts that are made at the factory. But a bike still needs other parts such as chains, brakes, pedals, seats, and handlebars. The bike factory buys the parts from other companies that manufacture them.

Bikes are put together by a team of workers on an assembly line. The painted frames, forks, and wheels travel along a conveyor belt. The conveyor belt moves the parts past each assembly line worker, and he or she adds a different part. This process is much faster than if every worker put together an entire bike.

People on an assembly line must work quickly, as the bicycle frames and parts speed by.

Each person on an assembly line completes a different task. This worker is installing bearings, so that the bicycle's cranks and pedals can be attached.

The first worker on the assembly line installs the **headset,** the set of bearings and bearing cups that allow the handlebars and fork to rotate. The next worker slides the fork into the frame's head tube and joins them with a nut.

Another worker attaches the crank axle sprockets and crank arms to the frame. The crank arms are what the pedals will be attached to later. Now brakes are attached. If the bike is one with shifters, the gear levers will go on next. They are followed by the cables, gears, chain, and the rear wheel.

A quality control inspector checks the bike. He or she spins the wheels and checks the pedals and brakes. If any parts are damaged or the bike doesn't work, the bike can't be sold as it is. Whatever is wrong with the bike must be fixed.

The inspector also checks for nicks and dents. Nicked or dented bikes may be sold to the bike factory workers at a special discount. Some companies sell these to the public at a lower price, too.

Each bicycle is inspected before it leaves the factory.

The partially assembled bicycle is carefully packed and shipped to a store, where it will be finished.

When bicycles come off the assembly line, they usually don't have pedals, handlebars, seats, kickstands, or front wheels. These parts will be put in at the shop where the bikes are sold. They're packed into a separate box or bag, along with an instruction book for assembling the bike.

Finally, the bike is put into a box and loaded onto a truck. Soon you'll see it in a shop window on display.

1

At the Shop

Wherever you buy a bike, it's best to purchase one that's already assembled. Many bike shops won't even sell unassembled bikes. They have an agreement with the manufacturers they buy from that only fully assembled bikes can leave the shop. Both the manufacturers and the shops want their bicycles to be properly assembled by bicycle mechanics. That way, you'll be sure to buy a bike that works well.

After a bike arrives at a store, a mechanic opens the box and checks that it contains all the parts. Then the mechanic begins putting the bike together.

Putting together a bicycle takes about one hour and about 18 different tools.

Left: *Attaching the front wheel.*
Below: *Taping the handlebars.*

To begin, the partially assembled bike is clamped into the service stand—a pole that lifts the bike a few feet off the ground. When the bike is raised, it's easier for the mechanic to work on it.

The mechanic attaches the front wheel to the frame and fork with screws, and with washers—small disks that make the screws tight. Handlebars are installed next. The mechanic greases the handlebars well and slides them into place. Rubber handlebar grips are slipped on, or the handlebars are wrapped with tape.

Now the mechanic installs the seat onto the seat post—the adjustable part that raises and lowers the seat. When the seat and post are joined, the seat post is greased and inserted into the seat tube. The seat post is secured with bolts.

If the bike is one with hand brakes, the cables are connected now. Wires inside the cable are pulled from the cable's plastic housing, stretched, and cut. Then they're locked into the **caliper brakes**—the horseshoe-shaped device on the bike's wheel. The mechanic makes sure the pads on the caliper hug the wheel rim. If they don't, the brakes won't work correctly.

Above: *Installing the seat.* Left: *Connecting the brake cables.*

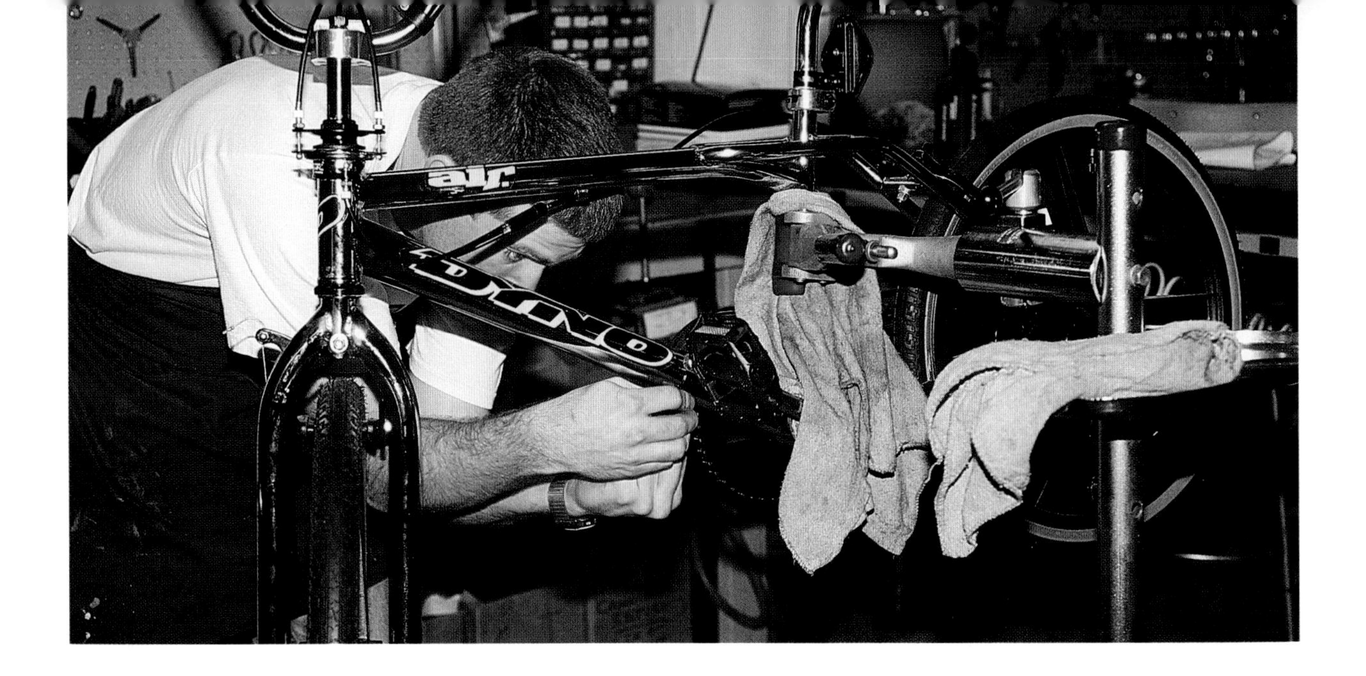

A bicycle mechanic makes a few final adjustments before a bike leaves the store.

The mechanic attaches the pedals to the cranks, installs wheel reflectors, and adjusts the gears. If necessary, the mechanic also trues the wheels again. Even though the wheels were trued at the factory, spokes can come loose when they've been jiggled around on a truck. Tires may lose a little air on the truck, too. So the mechanic may also inflate the tires.

At last the bike is ready to put on display. But before you take it out of the shop, a mechanic checks it over one more time and adjusts the bike so that it's just your size. For the miles of riding ahead, it's important your bike be a perfect fit.

8

Bike Care

Your bike will last for years with good care. Here are some tips to help it run smoothly and look terrific:

1. Keep your bike out of the rain, or the unpainted parts can rust. Park it in a dry, safe place such as your garage, basement, or even inside the house.

2. Clean your bike once a month with a damp, soft rag. Wipe the tires, too. Tiny stones and bits of dirt get caught in the tires' grooves.

3. Don't ride your bike over curbs, and avoid skidding. These actions deflate and weaken the tires, and jolt your wheels' mechanisms.

4. Keep your tires fully inflated, with a foot or hand pump that's made for bikes. Gas station pumps are made for cars, not bikes. It's very easy to blow out your tires with a car-tire pump.

5. Oil your bike's chain, nuts and bolts, hubs, and brakes once a month. Use only bike oil from a bike shop. To oil hubs, squeeze about two drops of oil into the oil hole and wipe off the excess. Lightly oil other nuts and bolts. To oil the chain, clean it first with a damp rag. Then turn the pedals very slowly. Put a drop of oil on each section, then wipe it off. This should be done any time your bike gets wet.

6. Before each ride, look over your gears, brakes, seat, and pedals. They need to be tight. If they are loose, tighten them with a wrench. It just takes a few seconds, and it's worth it to be safe.

7. When storing your bike for more than a week, hang it on a hook, or turn it upside down. This will keep the tires from deflating.

9 Repairs

No matter how well you take care of your bike, parts will break or wear out. You shouldn't try to fix gears or brakes. They are complicated, and if you don't fix them correctly, you could have to replace them or pay for expensive shop repairs later. But you can make some simple repairs yourself. The tools you'll need are available at any bike shop.

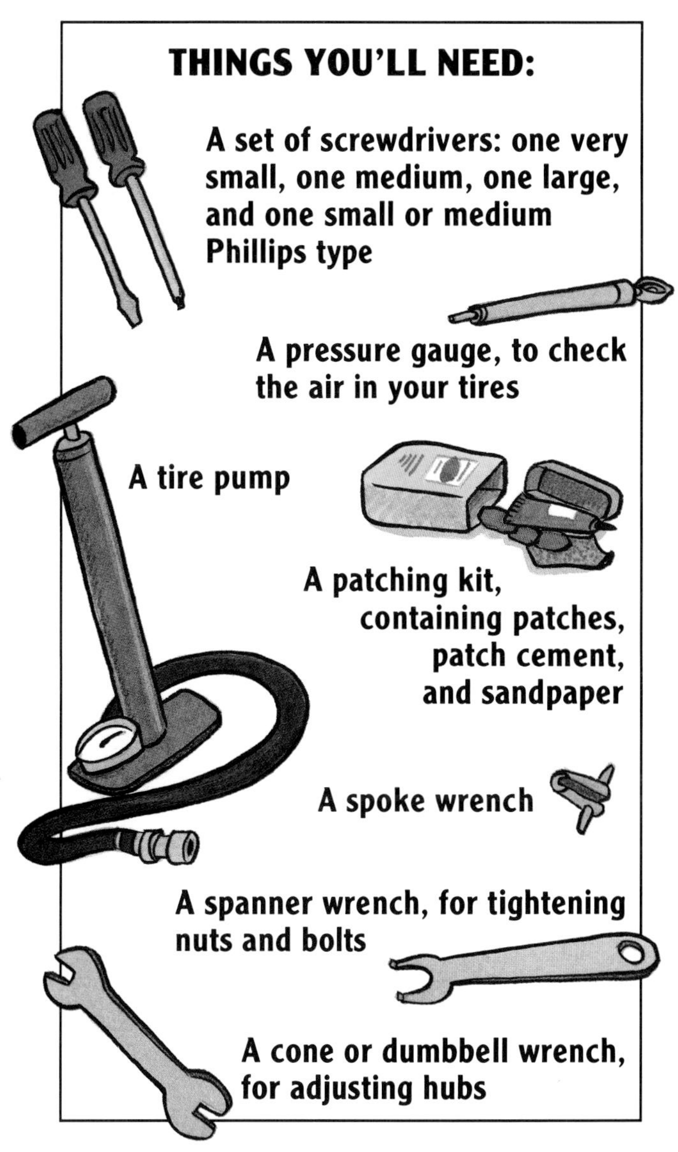

THINGS YOU'LL NEED:

- A set of screwdrivers: one very small, one medium, one large, and one small or medium Phillips type
- A pressure gauge, to check the air in your tires
- A tire pump
- A patching kit, containing patches, patch cement, and sandpaper
- A spoke wrench
- A spanner wrench, for tightening nuts and bolts
- A cone or dumbbell wrench, for adjusting hubs

CHAINS

Sometimes the chain slips off the sprocket. It's easy to repair.

Replacing a chain:

1. Remove the chain completely from the large front sprocket.
2. Make sure the chain is attached to the small back sprocket teeth. (If it isn't attached, you'll need to take your bike to a shop.)
3. Put a few chain links on the front sprocket's teeth.
4. Turn the pedals forward while you hold on to the chain links in the front sprocket. The chain should slip on.

SPOKES

If you have lots of loose spokes, take your bike to the shop. Loose spokes may be a sign of other, more serious problems. But you can fix up to five spokes yourself. Here's how:

Fixing loose spokes:

1. Lay your bike on the ground. Rest it on its seat and handlebars.

2. Fit the spoke wrench around the spoke nipple and twist.
3. Hit the spoke with your finger to make sure it's tight. If you hear a high-pitched ping, it's tight. A lower-pitched sound means it still needs tightening.

TIRES

Changing tires is a big job—one for the repair shop or for an experienced adult. But you can learn to patch a tube leak or inflate a tire yourself.

Patching a tube leak:

1. With sandpaper from the patch kit, sand around the hole, about one inch on all sides.
2. Spread glue on the sanded area.
3. Peel the backing from the patch. Press the patch over the hole.

Inflating a tire:

1. Unscrew the valve cap.
2. Insert pump nozzle over cap.
3. Pump just until the tire feels firm. (Don't over-inflate, or your tire will explode.)

BIKE SAFETY

- Wear a helmet.
- Wear bright colors and use reflectors on your clothing and bike.
- Don't ride on busy streets.
- Stop at all stop signs and red lights.
- Pay attention to the cars around you.
- Always stop and check for cars before entering a street from your driveway.
- Ride with traffic, not against it.
- Don't ride at night.
- Unless your bike is a tandem (having more than one seat), don't carry any passengers.
- Before turning left, look back and wait for traffic behind you and oncoming traffic to pass.
- Don't do any trick riding, unless you're on a dirt track and using a dirt bike.
- Ride in a straight line—don't swerve. If you need to change directions, use hand signals.

ball bearing: a rolling metal ball that allows two pieces of metal to slide against each other

blueprint: a diagram of the plans for building a bicycle, car, building, or something else

caliper brakes: the horseshoe-shaped device on a bicycle's back wheel. Caliper brakes apply pressure to either side of the back wheel when hand brakes are applied, stopping the bike.

chain drive: the system of pedal cranks, sprockets, and chain that together power a bicycle

chrome: chromium, a very hard metal that doesn't rust easily. It is often used to plate (coat) other metals.

coaster brakes: brakes that stop a bike when the rider backpedals

Computer-Aided Design (CAD): a type of drawing used by designers, including the mechanical engineers who design bicycles. With computer programs, engineers create pictures or diagrams of a new bicycle. The programs then solve equations to predict how the bicycle will work.

fork: the part of a bicycle that joins the front wheel to the frame

headset: the set of bearings that allow a bicycle's handlebars and fork to rotate

hub: the center part of a wheel

pneumatic (noo-MAT-ik) tires: tires filled with air

primer: a coat of paint that smoothes a surface and prepares it for a second coat

prototype: the first sample of a new product, such as a new style of bicycle

rim: the outer part of a wheel. The rim is attached to the wheel hub with spokes.

spokes: braces that join a wheel's hub to its rim

sprocket: a toothed wheel

true: to make straight. To true a bicycle wheel is to straighten any bumps or bends in the rim.

weld: to permanently join two pieces of metal with a metal filler

INDEX

ACKNOWLEDGMENTS

This book would not have been possible without the generous help of the following people and organizations:

Ed Sutter, Engineering Manager, Roadmaster Bicycle Corporation; Richard Buzek, Head Mechanic, Rudy's Schwinn Shop, Lincolnwood, Illinois; Greg Grotch, Manager, Rudy's Schwinn Shop; Shawn Koukal, Mechanic, Rudy's Schwinn Shop; Trek Bicycle Corporation; and The Bicycle Institute of America.

The photographs in this book are reproduced through the courtesy of:

pp. 2, 14, 17, 18 (top), 22, 24, 27, Trek® Bicycle Corporation; pp. 6, 13, 21, Private Eye Photography, ©1992 by Karelle Scharff; pp. 8, 9, The British Library; p. 10, Smithsonian Institution; p. 11, Library of Congress; pp. 18 (bottom), 19, 29, Derby Cycle Corporation; pp. 30, 31, Derby Cycle Corporation, by Dan Lamont; pp. 20, 23, Cannondale Corporation; p. 28, The Bicycle Corporation of America; pp. 32, 33, 34 (both), 35 (both), 36, Fridley-Heights Cyclery, by Kathy Raskob/IPS.

Front cover photograph courtesy of Trek® Bicycle Corporation.
Back cover photograph by Carlye Calvin.

ABOUT THE AUTHOR

Arlene Erlbach has written more than a dozen books of fiction and nonfiction for young people. In addition to being an author, she is an elementary school teacher. She loves to encourage children to read and write, and she is in charge of her school's Young Authors' program. Ms. Erlbach lives in Morton Grove, Illinois, with her husband, her son, a collie, and three cats.